PIANO / CELLO
THE PIANO GUYS -

MW00860555

Photos courtesy The Piano Guys

Folio concept by Craig Knudsen

ISBN 978-1-70515-564-6

Visit Hal Leonard Online at
www.halleonard.com

Contact us:
Hal Leonard
7777 West Bluemound Road
Milwaukee, WI 53213
Email: info@halleonard.com

In Europe, contact:
Hal Leonard Europe Limited
42 Wigmore Street
Marylebone, London, W1U 2RN
Email: info@halleonardeurope.com

In Australia, contact:
Hal Leonard Australia Pty. Ltd.
4 Lentara Court
Cheltenham, Victoria, 3192 Australia
Email: info@halleonard.com.au

Before You Go

Abraham Lincoln

Anyone

Sweet Child O

CONTENTS

"My Girl" arranged by Al van der Beek, David Tolk,
Phillip Keveren and Steven Sharp Nelson.
QR code omitted due to licensing restrictions.

Paul

Steve

Jon

Al

As performed by The Piano Guys

MY GIRL

Words and Music by SMOKEY ROBINSON
and RONALD WHITE

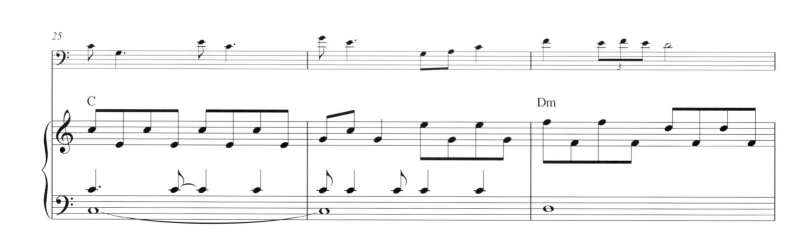

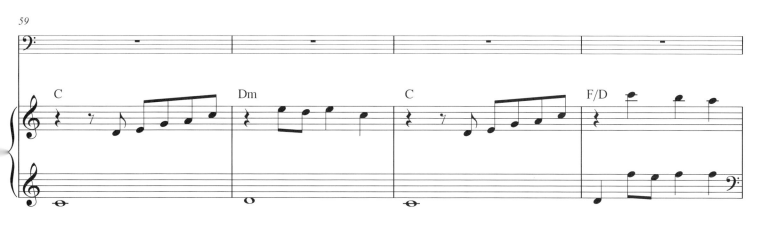

8va if possible through m. 76

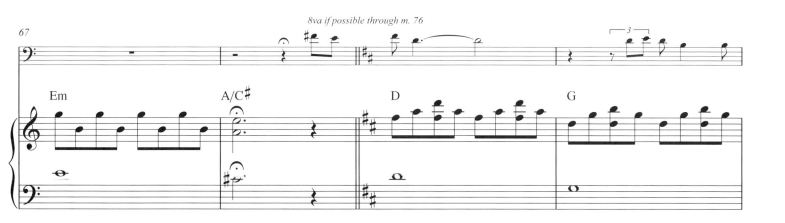

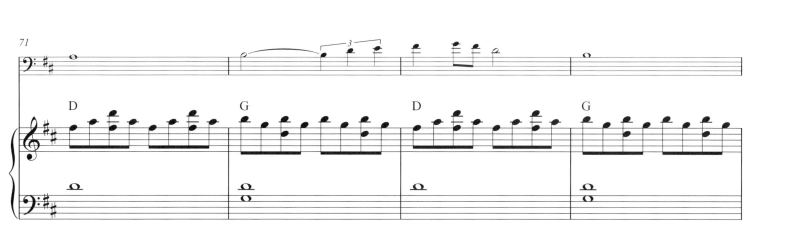

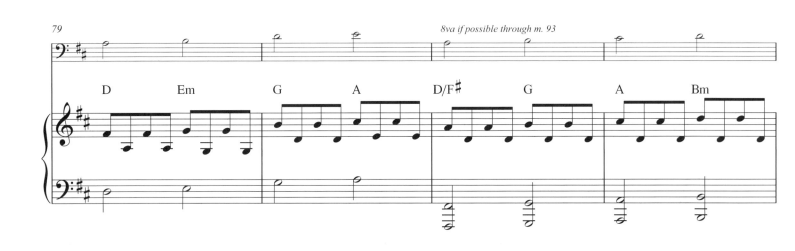

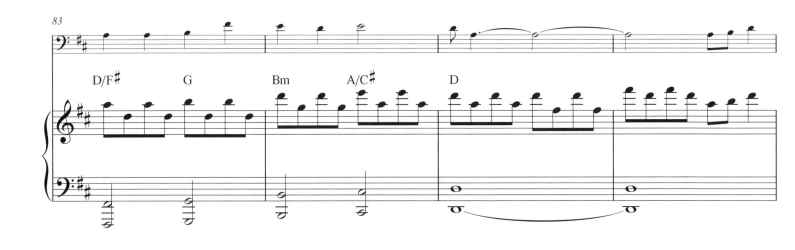

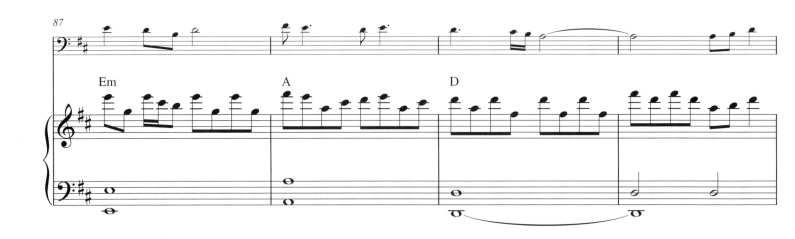

As performed by The Piano Guys

WAKE ME UP BEFORE YOU GO-GO

Words and Music by
GEORGE MICHAEL
Arranged by Al van der Beek
and Steven Sharp Nelson

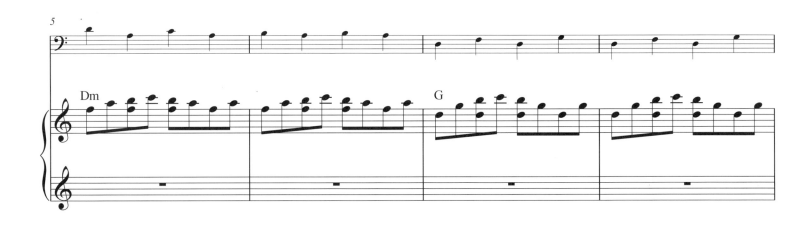

As performed by The Piano Guys

SOMEONE LIKE YOU

Words and Music by ADELE ADKINS
and DAN WILSON
Arranged by Al van der Beek,
Marshall McDonald and Steven Sharp Nelson

Watch video

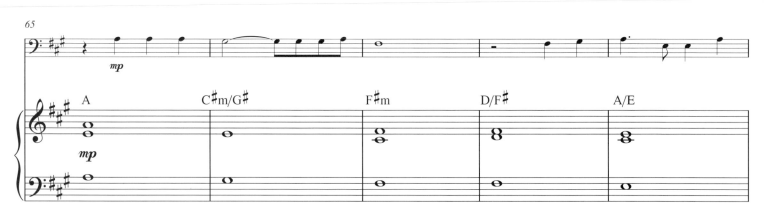

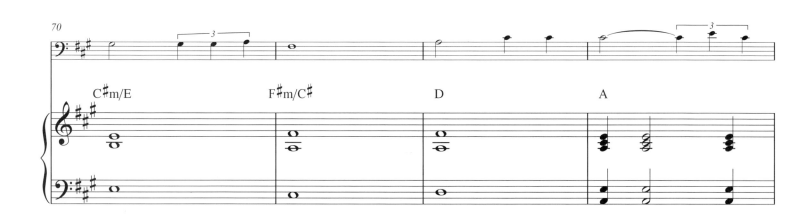

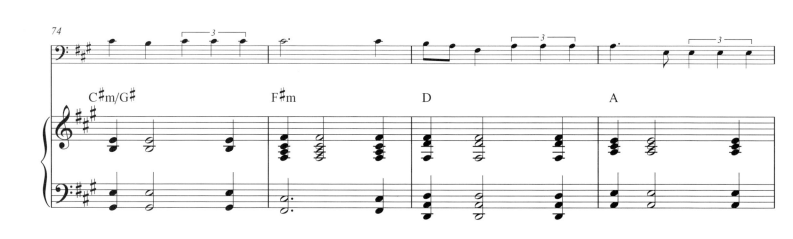

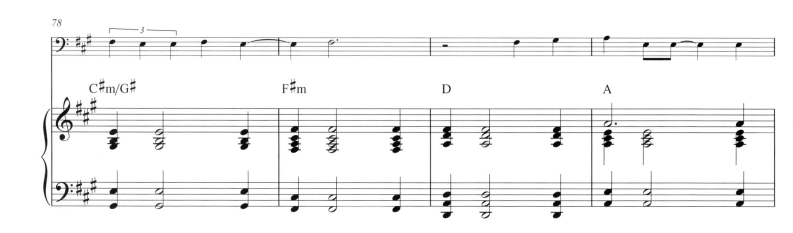

As performed by The Piano Guys

STRESSED OUT

Words and Music by
TYLER JOSEPH
Arranged by Al van der Beek
and Steven Sharp Nelson

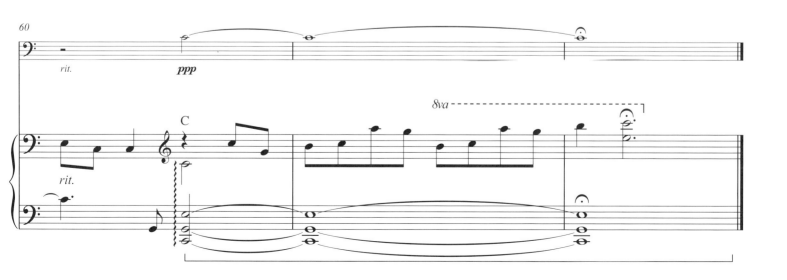

As performed by The Piano Guys

SWEET CHILD O' MINE

Words and Music by W. AXL ROSE,
SLASH, IZZY STRADLIN',
DUFF McKAGAN and STEVEN ADLER
Arranged by Al van der Beek,
David Tolk, Phillip Keveren,
and Steven Sharp Nelson

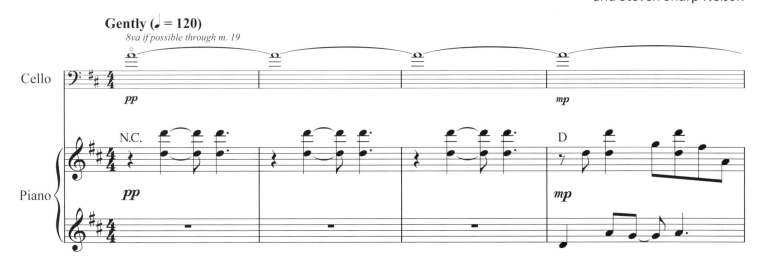

8va if possible through m. 43

I WILL ALWAYS LOVE YOU

Words and Music by
DOLLY PARTON
Arranged by Al van der Beek,
Marshall McDonald and Steven Sharp Nelson

As performed by The Piano Guys

JUPITER

By GUSTAV HOLST
Arranged by Steven Sharp Nelson
and Marshall McDonald

Slowly, expressively

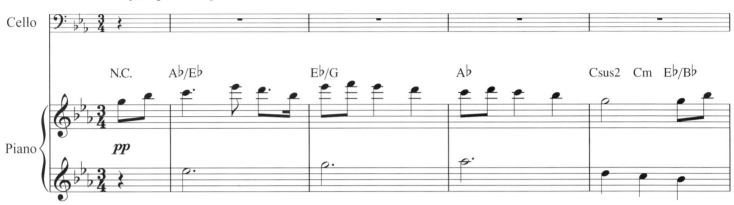

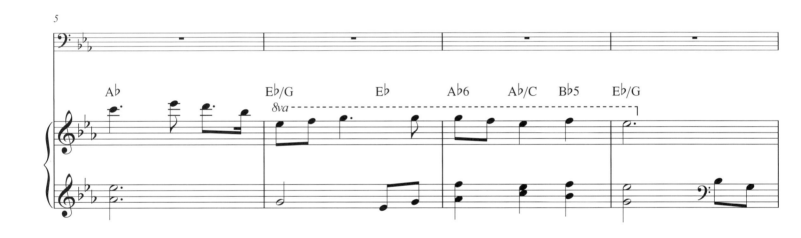

As performed by The Piano Guys

ABRAHAM LINCOLN TRIBUTE

Incorporates "Battle Hymn Of The Republic" by WILLIAM STEFFE and
"Nearer My God To Thee" by LOWELL MASON
Arranged by Al van der Beek
and Steven Sharp Nelson

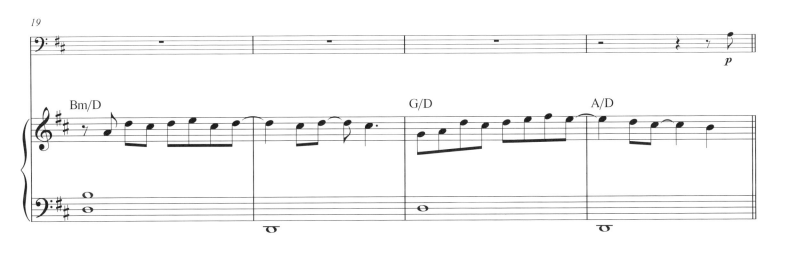

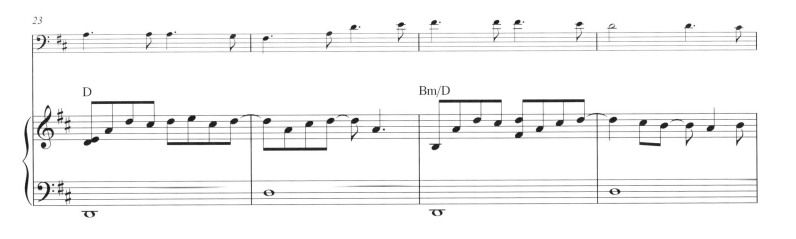

As performed by The Piano Guys

BEFORE YOU GO

Words and Music by LEWIS CAPALDI,
BENJAMIN KOHN, PETER KELLEHER,
THOMAS BARNES and PHILIP PLESTED
Arranged by Steven Sharp Nelson
and Al van der Beek

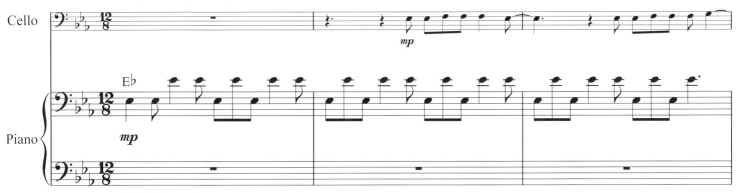

As performed by The Piano Guys

UNCHAINED MELODY
from the Motion Picture UNCHAINED

Lyric by HY ZARET
Music by ALEX NORTH
Arranged by Phillip Keveren,
Craig Knudsen, Al van der Beek
and Steven Sharp Nelson

As performed by The Piano Guys

GROW AS WE GO

Words and Music by BEN ABRAHAM,
ALEX HOPE and BEN PLATT
Arranged by Stephen Nelson
and Steven Sharp Nelson

Gentle Ballad (♩ = 81)

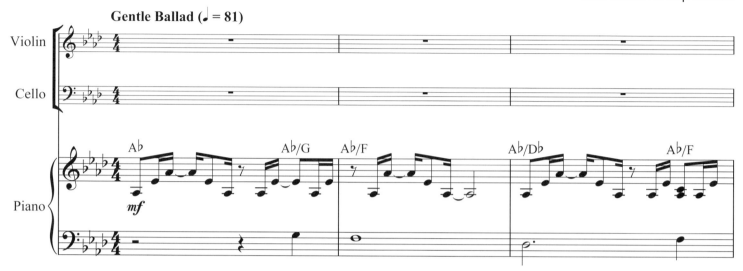

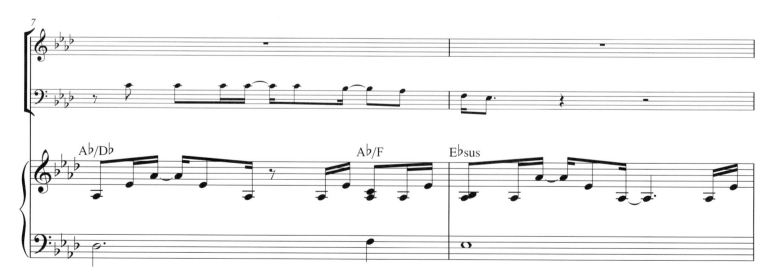

As performed by The Piano Guys

ANYONE

Words and Music by JUSTIN BIEBER,
JON BELLION, JORDAN JOHNSON,
ALEXANDER IZQUIERDO, ANDREW WATT,
RAUL CUBINA, STEFAN JOHNSON
and MICHAEL POLLACK
Arranged by Jon Schmidt,
Al van der Beek and Steven Sharp Nelson

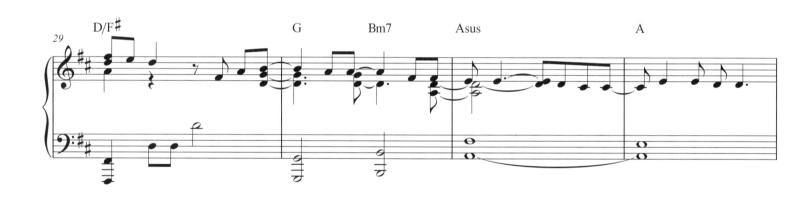

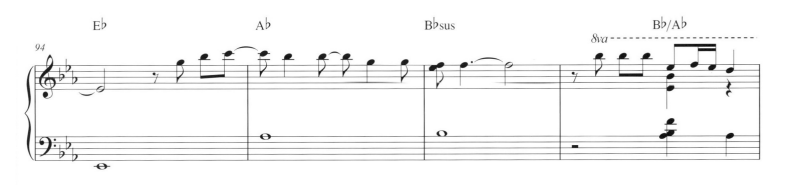

As performed by The Piano Guys

YOU ARE THE REASON

Inspired by Chopin Nocturne Op. 9 No. 2

Words and Music by CALUM SCOTT,
COREY SANDERS and JONATHAN MAGUIRE
Arranged by Kyle Pedunz,
Nathan Girard and Steven Sharp Nelson

Moderately

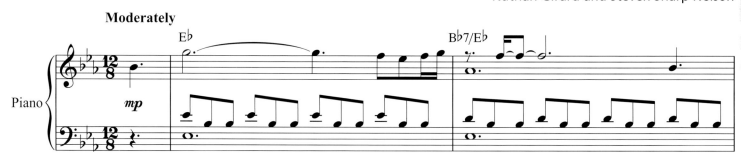

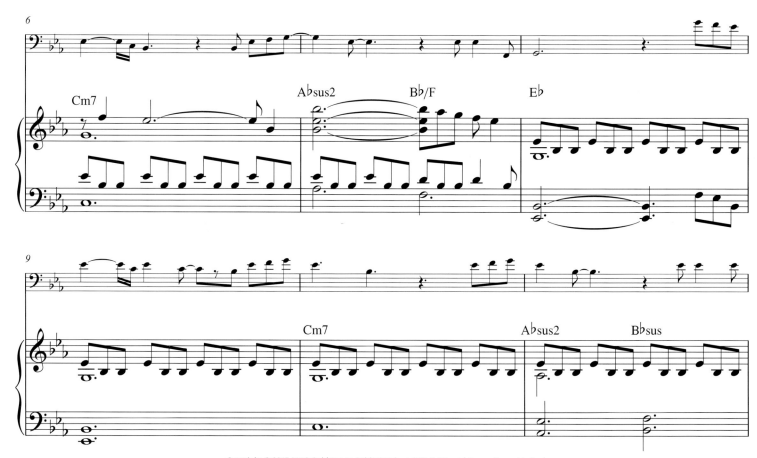